Watch Out!

Written by Barrie Wade
Illustrated by John Blackman

Collins *Educational*
An imprint of HarperCollins *Publishers*

The young mouse went out for the first time.
"Watch out for your enemy," said the old mouse.

"Help! Help!" the young mouse cried.
"I saw my enemy! He flapped his wings and screamed at me!"

"That was only the cock," the old mouse said.
"He will not hurt you. Watch out for your enemy."

Cock-a-doodle do!
Cock-a-doodle do!

Hee-haw!
Hee-haw!

"Help! Help!" the young mouse cried.
"I saw my enemy! She showed her teeth and roared at me!"

"That was only the donkey," the old mouse said.
"She will not hurt you. Watch out for your enemy."

Moo-oo!
Moo-oo!

"Help! Help!" the young mouse cried.
"I saw my enemy! He stamped his foot and bellowed at me."

"That was only the bull," the old mouse said.
"He will not hurt you. Watch out for your enemy."

"But who is my enemy?" asked the young mouse.

"I cannot speak her name," replied the old mouse, "but she has golden eyes and fur as soft as silk."

“Will she scream or roar or bellow at me?” asked the young mouse.

“No, her voice is gentle,” answered the old mouse, “and she moves as silently as thinking.”

“Then she is nothing to be scared of,” said the young mouse.

“So you may think,” said the old mouse. “But watch out!”